Her

A Voice Within

Charvi

Made with ❤ on the BookLeaf Publishing Platform

www.bookleafpub.in

www.bookleafpub.com

Dedication

This book is dedicated to my mother and uncle, who never stopped believing in me and loves me unconditionally.

It is also dedicated to all the seekers who have ever felt lost.

May you always find the courage to listen to the voice within,

and may it lead you home.

Preface

There comes a time in life when we begin to question everything—our purpose, our identity and the meaning behind the moments that shape us. This book was born from that search.

Her – A Voice Within is not just a collection of words; it is a reflection of the inner dialogue we all have but often ignore. It is the voice that speaks to us in silence, in longing, in self-doubt and in transformation. This book is deeply personal, yet it belongs to everyone who has ever felt lost and longed to be found.

Writing this was not just a process but a journey— one that led me to understand that the answers we seek are not hidden in the world but within ourselves. Aurelia's journey mirrors that of many— seeking love, purpose and belonging—only to realise that home has always been within.

This is not a book that gives instructions or tells you what to believe. Instead, it offers perspectives, questions and emotions that you may recognise in your own life. Some passages may speak to you instantly, while others may take time to settle in your heart.

If this book finds you at a crossroad, I hope it serves as a companion. If it finds you in stillness, I hope it whispers truths you have long known but never put into words. And if it finds you searching, may it remind you that the journey itself is the destination.

Let this book be an open door—step in, pause and listen to your own voice within.

Acknowledgements

To Akshat, who encouraged me to take a step forward and provided constant support throughout and to Asad, whose designing skills have been invaluable.
A heartfelt thank you to my dear friends for giving it an unreleased read—Neha, Suchitra and Prashanthi.
To all the seekers and to every reader who finds a piece of themselves in these pages—this book is for you.

CHAPTER ONE

THE AWAKENING

The night was still. It was not the peaceful kind, but the kind that hung around, heavy and observant; waiting for something to shatter. The air was heavy with the smell of rain that never fell, the type that bewitched the ground but refused to fall.

Aurelia was seated cross-legged on the floor, gazing at the mirror before her. It was not just glass—it was a border, a delicate separation between all she had ever known and something unknown. Something waiting to be discovered.

Though her breathing was even, her fingers were shaking a little as she stretched out. The surface was chilly and hard. Her face stared back with the same eyes, same face and same quiet and yet... There was something different, almost as though the mirror was not merely revealing her, but observing her.

"Is this where it begins?"

She had always sensed that heaviness in her chest, that unspoken tug towards something outside the world she was familiar with. A voice inside her that never belonged to this world. A whisper that reminded her that she was more than her body or her name, more than all the years that had etched themselves into her life.

But she never heard it...

Until now.

The First Realization

There is a moment when a soul awakens—not from slumber, but from a trance. It is at this instant, doubts are louder than truths and the world no longer holds the shape it was moulded in. This is the spark of the start.

Aurelia had seen the truth and once she glimpsed beyond the veil, there was no going back.

The candle flame next to her flickered, the shadows dancing across the walls. The room seemed to shrink and the air thickened. She was no longer thinking. She was feeling and that was the deadliest thing of all.

She took a deep breath, opened her eyes and focused.

The time had come.

This was not just a night. This was the beginning.

She set her palm flat on the mirror.

A sudden, cold prickly feeling coursed through her fingers. The mirror wavered like it was made of water.

Her image became hazy, the edges of her face fading into something unfamiliar.

And then, silence.

The Moment of Departure

She had never been lost, merely waiting, merely poised at the rim of something vast.

But tonight, she hesitated not.

She reached out.

And the world turned.

Aurelia gasped, jerking her hand back. The mirror was no longer a mirror.

It was a doorway. A window into something deeper than she could understand.

For the first time in her life, she wasn't scared of what lay on the other side.

She took a step forward.

And the journey started.

CHAPTER TWO

ECHO OF FOREVERMORE

The night spread itself across the world like a boundless, infinite sea. Aurelia, though, did not move. She stared into the silence, where only her mind spoke.

She had been told all along that love was easy, it was a thing that lingered, flourished and never departed. But tonight, she wondered if that was true. Was love ever truly eternal? Or was it just an echo? Fading far away, a haunting refrain that never belonged to anyone.

She had known love in its various guises. She had felt its hot fury, its icy withdrawal. There had been burning hands and golden words that bored into her skin. And yet, all of it had come to nothing in the end.

The past was like a song she could no longer hear but still knew the words to.

Love had been a storm, a bold flight, an unmade wish

and yet, here she was, fate's cruel joke.

Is it just the fate of all things bardic to flourish and wither?

The Silence That Held Her

Others were saying that love never dies. But love, it changes, it clings, it resonates. She had pursued it, begged it, attempted to mould it into something that would be hers. But love was never something you could possess. It was something that was supposed to be lived and let go of.

Aurelia rolled onto her side, fingers tracing her pillow. Memories danced like candlelight, soft, warm and vanishing with each inhale.

"Am I lost in this? Or am I finally free?"

She had spent too many nights looking for answers elsewhere. Tonight, she looked for them inside herself.

Love shouldn't be hunger. It shouldn't be the fire that burns and leaves only ashes to remain.

She had seen others cling to it like a mirage, wishing on stars, borrowing time. But she no longer wanted these things. She desired something whole, still, unbound.

The Strength of Letting Go

She walked streets that echoed tears, through empty

halls where love used to sleep. No longer pursuing, begging, blind. But love must never submit. Its echoes no longer clung to her. They were now the property of time, floating in the abyss of what used to be. She had carried them long enough. Now, she would hold herself.

The stars flickered unchangingly, yet constant. They witnessed all her rises and falls. And still, they remained, unsoiled by the tumult of human desire.

Maybe love isn't about holding on. Perhaps it is about letting the echoes live, but not letting them define you.

She was not broken. She was not lost. She was simply someone who had learnt that love is not the weight of want. It is not a prison. It is not a fire that devours. It is a thing that must breathe. And leave if it must.

For what is supposed to stay will never be kept by force. And what is not supposed to stay will only take bits of you when you beg it to.

Aurelia breathed, lighter than she had been in years.

Love had marked her, but no longer possessed her.

She would sleep now.

And she would rise again.

And in the morning, the whispers of forevermore would no longer be something she bore. They would merely be something she allowed.

CHAPTER THREE

The Weight of Want

Night had not yet fallen, yet Aurelia's thoughts pummelled against her skull, pushing into the silence like an unasked question.

She was a stillness, her eyes moving over the shadows that ran along the walls, the city's distant hum of light, a gentle thrum. Want had always been an unsettled something within her. A hunger. A yearning. A whisper that refused to stop.

She had spent years pursuing the concept of fulfilment, thinking that if she could only clutch something close for long enough, keep it tight enough, make it hers, the pain would at last disappear.

But now she questioned whether she had been looking for something real or had just been pursuing an illusion.

The Illusion of Desire

Desire is a fleeting thing. It burns hot but never remains. It promises but never delivers. It is a hunger for love and a longing for truth.

She knew its weight—the pain of longing, the pursuit of something always just out of reach. But had she ever really paused to wonder? Was it meant to be grasped? Or was it only meant to be experienced?

The Lover That Never Stayed

She rolled over, her fingertips drawing patterns into the weave of her sheets.

She had encountered him where lanterns breathed and city air meshed with night. A silk-and-sin world where love was in short supply, but desire was lean.

His voice had been velvet, dark and deep—a breathed vow she didn't dare uphold.

His hands were fire, wild, unfettered, but never stayed. They danced where shadows gently undulated, where quiet promises would later betray.

He etched his name on her skin, but love was nowhere to start.

She had confused intensity with something more.

Confused passion with longevity.

Now, she recognised it for what it was—a flash, a spark,

an instant. Never a forever.

The Ache of the Unfinished

Lust, a comet, flared and perished, a brief spark, a fiery life.

It flowered, it shattered, it scarred, a wish left unspoken, a star beyond reach.

She'd wasted too much time gazing upon love from a spectator in a huge theatre, seeing others play their roles, vowing forever on lips that had never spoken the truth.

She'd promised herself she'd never be like them.

And yet, hadn't she? Hadn't she allowed herself to believe? Hadn't she clung to something that never was hers to begin with?

She rolled over onto her back, gazing up at the ceiling.

"Am I still chasing? Am I still waiting?"

The Truth Beneath Want

Some desires are not meant to be satisfied. Some are intended only to instruct.

She had waited years, sought, yearned for something that could not be grasped. And perhaps, she was ready to let go.

The Kind of Love That Remained

And then there was the evening she encountered someone different.

He was not a flame. He was not a tempest. He did not pursue, he did not beg. He did not push against her like a fire, requiring to be fueled.

Rather, he was at peace. His voice was calm, his hands gentle. He was not a craving, not a hunger. He did not fill a void; he never meant to in the first place...

And in this stillness, something bloomed.

Not wildfire passion, not frantic longing. But something complete, something true.

No burning fingers, no breathed entreaties, no broken hearts on bended knees.

But something entire, where longing ended, a love that did not beg for peace.

She turned to him one evening, observing the evenness of his breathing as he slept.

He never held her back.

And so, for the first time, she stayed.

The Weight She Had Finally Released

Aurelia let go of a deep breath, shutting her eyes.

"I will not pursue ghosts."

"I will not confuse want for love."

She had borne the burden of desire for too long. But now, she knew love was not the weight she dreaded, it was not starvation, not a flame that devoured.

It was something constant, something permanent. Something that did not have to be held white knuckled, because it had always been intended to remain.

Some will pursue forever. Some will wait for something that was never meant to be theirs.

But she—she had learned. Learned that love is not something to be held on to, but something to be welcomed with open hands.

And in that still place, where yearning dwelt, she had at last achieved peace.

CHAPTER FOUR

THE MIRROR

The evening was silent, but Aurelia felt the pressure of
the day bearing down on her mind. The quietness of the
world did not translate to quietness in her; it amplified
her thoughts to be louder, clearer, more merciless.
She sat on the edge of her bed, looking at the mirror in
the other room. A reflection was meant to be easy. A
surface, an image, a truth revealed. But tonight, she
wasn't certain if what she saw was the truth or another
deception.
Some nights, she knew herself.
Some nights, she didn't.

The Truth in Reflection

*A mirror never lies. It never bends, never softens, never
comforts. It only shows the truth. But then, the question
is—what does one see?*

Some see their past. Some see their pain. Some see a stranger in their skin.

And Aurelia sees something vast, something moving, something waiting to be figured out.

She leaned in, her breath misting against the chilled glass.

Her eyes were the same. But was she?

She had taken years to fixing her hair, altering her stance, learning how to present herself, so the world might comprehend. But had she ever really looked at herself?

Or had she simply looked at the version she was taught to be?

The Shadow of Self-doubt

Somewhere deep within, there was a part of her that doubted everything. The decisions she had made. The roads she had travelled. The voice within her sometimes sounded strange, like it was not hers at all.

Who was she?

The world had provided her with a thousand responses. Daughter. Lover. Dreamer. Seeker.

But none of them seemed sufficient. None of them seemed complete.

She lightly touched the mirror, following the line of her own face. "Who am I when no one is looking?"

The mirror did not reply.

It only reflected what she already knew but had been too scared to say she was still looking.

Beyond the Glass, Beyond the Surface

The mirror observed but never spoke; it never cracked, it never shattered.

It contained her shape but not her fire, for deeper called the cosmic name.

Past her image, past the thin skin she had worn for so long, she felt it—a presence, a self that is greater than the self.

It was not her body.

Not her history.

Not the scars she bore.

It was something larger. Something unmarred by time, by definition, by expectation.

She shut her eyes, feeling it in her bones.

She wasn't merely the shape. She was the light.

The Past That Still Remained

Memories danced at the periphery of her mind—

moments when she'd doubted, times when she'd fallen,

decisions she'd wanted to erase.

She'd wasted too much time pursuing reflections,

attempting to construct something they never were.

Not skin or bone, neither loss nor gain. Not fleeting joy or earthly pain.

Her past had attempted to define her.

Her errors had attempted to claim her.

But she was coming to realise she was greater than the things that she had lost.

Greater than the things she had feared.

The Universe Within Her

She was not what faded with the years,

Not just her laughter. Not just her tears.

She was the vast, the deep, the whole, the universe wrapped in a mortal soul.

She exhaled a slow breath, observing her image change in the faint light.

No longer defined by one instant, one definition of herself.

She was infinite. Spreading. *Becoming.*

The mirror would forever exist, reflecting what the world needed to see.

But now she knew better.

She was not merely her image. She was the light it reflected.

And that reality is unshatterable.

CHAPTER FIVE

SILENCE

The evening enfolded Aurelia in its gentle grasp, not oppressive, not smothering—just quiet.

She reclined in bed, eyes shut, listening. To nothing. To everything.

Silence had patiently waited all along, but she had spent the majority of her existence covering it— with sound, with ideas, with distractions. She had been afraid of what it would say if she allowed it to settle.

But tonight, she did not flee from it.

She allowed it to be.

She allowed herself to be in it.

The Language of Silence

Most fear silence. They confuse it with emptiness, with loneliness. But silence is not absence—it is presence. It is space. It is depth.

In silence, the world does not vanish. It is only heard differently.
And those who dare to listen, those who hold dear the quiet, will discover that silence speaks in ways the world never can.

The Calm Within Her

She breathed in, deep and slow, feeling her breath fill in her chest.
She was not lost.
She was not agitated.
For the first time in years, she was simply here.
She had searched for answers for years in other people's voices, in books, in whispers from the past.
But now, she saw answers don't come from the outer world's noise.
Some responses are born out of silence itself.

The Vastness of Stillness

The more I hold onto silence, the more peaceful I am.
Like a newborn bird inside me, looking for comfort, unaware of what lies ahead, uncaring about the past.
Only here.
Only now.
Only this moment is mine.

She rolled onto her side, observing the way the night stretched out endlessly beyond her window.

The world continued moving, always. But she no longer had to run after it.

Silence was not required.

It did not dominate.

It just was.

And with it around, she was.

The Power of Stillness

Most fill the silence with noise because they do not trust what it might reveal. But she— she had learned to trust it.

She had learned that within silence lies clarity. And within clarity lies peace.

And peace is not something to be discovered. It is something to be permitted.

She shut her eyes, the silence still vibrating around her like a wavering heartbeat.

She would get up tomorrow and the world would keep moving.

But this evening, she chose quietness.

And in the process, she discovered everything.

CHAPTER SIX

HIGH ON LIFE

The horizon yawned wide above Aurelia, open and endless, a canvas upon which the sun brushed its golden colours along the edge.

She sat on the rooftop, legs tucked under her, the wind cold where it creased through her hair. She was not pursuing. Not searching. Not attempting to repair the world or herself.

She was merely here.

Alive.

Breathing.

And for once in a while, that sufficed.

The Lightness of Being

Most spend their lives waiting for happiness, for love, for the perfect moment to arrive.

But she had learned that life is not something to be

waited for. It is something to be felt, to be lived, to be breathed in fully, without hesitation.

And when someone ceases waiting and begins to live, they discover that happiness has always existed in the plain, unassuming moments.

The Weight She Had Released

She had held so much.

Guilt. Regret. The pain of might-have-beens.

She had spent nights drowning in thoughts, attempting to rewrite history, attempting to see the future.

But tonight, under the sky that had no boundaries, she let go at last.

And in that release, she was lighter than ever before.

The Dance of the Present

High on life, I arise with the sunrise, a nomad under the boundless expanse.

No shackles of yesterday, no dread of tomorrow, only wind, only sun, only breathing in my body.

I am not waiting.

I am not lost.

I am here.

And that is all it takes. She smiled to herself, raising her eyes towards the scattered stars which had already begun to blink on in the sky.

The world would go on.

The days would go on.

And she—she would continue to opt for life.

Not yesterday.

Not tomorrow.

But here.

Now.

Always.

Happiness is not a destination. It is not something to be achieved. It is something to be felt in the in-between times, in the places where life occurs organically.

And she—she was no longer waiting. *She was living.*

Aurelia's gentle laugh swept away into the open sky on the breeze.

She was alive.

And for the first time, that was all she had to be.

CHAPTER SEVEN

TOUCH THE ESSENCE

It had fallen into the night with softness, enfolding the world in gentle quiet. Aurelia was in bed, running her fingers around the shape of her palm, tracing the feel of her skin.

Touch. The least loud, yet strongest feeling of union. She remembered the hands that had touched her life passing, the strong, the ones that remained, the ones who left. Each touch had left something, a memory, a lesson, an impression on her soul.

The Unseen Power of Touch

Some say love is in words, in promises, in grand gestures. But love— true, raw, unspoken love— is often found in the smallest touch.

A hand on your head, resting softly. A silent comfort in a world that's too loud. A warmth that says more than words ever can.

Touch doesn't lie. It has weight, meaning and intention. And in its presence, we belong.

The Touch That Healed

Aurelia shut her eyes, recalling the way her mother had held her when she was a child with protection not so much, but with understanding, with an unspoken vow that no matter how dark things got in the world, she'd always have somewhere to lay her head.

It was a touch that instilled her with love before she knew the words.

She had spent years believing love needed to be loud, needed to be claimed, needed to be pursued. But didn't love also exist in the quiet?

A hand laid softly over hers.

A forehead kissed in passing.

A heat beside her that never demanded anything back.

Wasn't that love, too?

The Soul's Imprint

We touch.

Not just skin. We touch in presence, in words not said.

In the spaces in between silences.

And when the touch is real, it does not disappear.

It remains.

It becomes.

It lingers.

She breathed out, laying her hand on her chest.

Had she touched the world as it had touched her?

Had she left something behind? Not in names, not in great deeds, but in the way she had made others feel.

She wished she had.

She wished to imagine that many years after she'd be no longer, someone would shut their eyes, feel warmth in recollection and recall that there was a time when she had been present here.

The deepest touch is not the one felt upon the skin, but the one left upon the soul.

Some will forget your words. Some will forget your face. But they will never forget the way you made them feel.

And that is what will endure.

Aurelia rolled onto her side, her fingers wrapping softly around something invisible.

She would sleep tonight, knowing that in her presence, in her words, in the quiet nature in which she lived—

She had made contact with the world.

And that, she knew, was sufficient.

CHAPTER EIGHT

COLOURS

Morning came softly, its light leaking through the window, colouring the wall's warm hues.

Aurelia woke from under the bedclothes, rubbing sleep away. The outside world was afire with colour, but not for the first time did she look.

She had known grey too long moments lost without substance, days passing indistinguishable from one to the next. But today she would see the world in colour.

With brightness.

With beauty.

With colour.

The Canvas of Existence

Most take their way through life without even noticing the colours that are everywhere around them. They look, but they never really see. They live, but they don't feel.

But those that stop, who see, will discover the world is
stained with the thousand hues of a miracle.
Each moment is a brushstroke. Each experience creates
depth. And when one opens their heart to see, life itself
is a masterpiece.

A Palette of Emotions

She went outside the morning breeze cooled on her skin.
The sky was stretched out in tones of pale blue, infinite
and inviting.
The trees whispered in green, their leaves dancing, alive,
vibrant.
The flowers were defiant in their stance, splashing reds,
oranges and yellows on the ground like frozen laughter
in bloom.
Even the shadows, which were once feared by her, now
held beauty in their depth.

The Inner Colours of the Soul

The world is not black and white.
It is every colour, every hue, painted not merely on the
sky, but in us as well.
Some days we shine golden, radiant, untamed.
Some days we blend into blue, soft, yearning, still.
But even on the greyest of days, the colours are there.

Waiting.

Hoping.

Waiting to be noticed.

The Colours She Chose to Wear

Aurelia smiled as she strolled, the sun's warmth against her skin.

She had spent too many days mired in the past, too many nights dreading the future.

But today she would live.

And today was coloured in light.

In color.

In potential.

Reflection

Others wait for joy, for love, for significance. But these things are found here, at this time, in the colours that exist.

She'd discovered that happiness is not found. It's something one elects.

And she—she was, at last, electing.

Aurelia breathed in deeply, letting the colours of the world find root within her heart.

She would keep them close to her.

She would colour her life in them.

And whatever the future was, she would never live in grey again.

28

CHAPTER NINE

WHAT I SEE

Night had fallen, folding the world in its soft darkness.
Aurelia was immobile, looking out into the shadows, her
mind sorting through the pictures of the day.
What did she see?
Not with her eyes, but with her spirit.
She had gazed at the world for so much of her life faces,
landscapes, at mirrors. But tonight, she wondered if she
had ever really looked.

The Illusion of Sight

Most think that to see is to know. But sight is an illusion.
The eyes take in pictures, but the heart defines them.
And at times, what the eyes reveal is not what exists.
Real sight is not seeing outwardly, but inwardly. It is not
seeing, but seeing.
And once one learns to see beyond appearance, the

world is never the same again.

The Shards of Perception

She remembered the ones she had met; their eyes full of things they never told, of feelings they kept locked away.
She had found beauty in fragments, strength in quiet, kindness in the unuttered.
She had seen the masks worn not for deception, but for survival.
And she had glimpsed herself in the faces of strangers- snatches of her past, fleeting moments of who she could have been in another life.

Beyond the Veil of Sight

I behold a world shrouded in gold, yet hidden underneath, a burden uncounted.
I behold faces chiselled in light, yet behind them, interminable night. I behold love that dares to flower, yet terror that confines it in darkness.
I behold.
But do I know?

The Moment of Realisation

She breathed out, turning onto her back and gazing at

the ceiling.

She had once been blind.

Blind to how the world whispered its secrets.

Blind to the depth that lay beneath plain moments.

Blind to the truth that what she was looking for was never outside—it was always inside.

"I see now."

Not with her eyes.

With her heart. With her soul. With the quiet knowing that only comes from seeing beyond the illusion.

And in that instant, she knew.

Most live their lives looking, but never seeing. But she— she had finally opened her eyes.

And now, the world would never be the same again.

Aurelia shut her eyes, but this time, she was not in darkness.

She could see everything. Clearly.

At last.

CHAPTER TEN

WHEN I SEE

The world hummed along at its normal speed hurtling, voices mixing, time falling through the fingers of things you couldn't see.

Aurelia stepped down the street, eyes awake, but she wasn't seeing it this time.

She was seeing.

She observed the details that everyone overlooked. The way the sky grew soft a moment before sunset, the way a kid clutched their parent's hand, a fraction of an inch tighter when they crossed the road, the way grief lurked behind manufactured smiles.

Things weren't what they appeared to be.

And once she saw, she knew.

The Conflict Between Eyes and Heart

Most live by sight, by what is set before them. But the

heart, the heart sees differently. The heart hears things the eyes ignore, catches the meaning in the silence, feels the weight of the unspoken.

And when one learns to trust what is felt rather than what is seen, the world unfolds in ways unimaginable.

The Truth in Every Moment

She walked by a woman alone at a coffee shop, gazing into her cup of coffee as if it contained the answers.

She walked by a boy laughing, but his eyes told a loneliness that his voice would never confess.

She walked by an old man reading a newspaper, his hands shaking, the wedding band loose on his thinning fingers.

The world pretended to go on.

But when she leaned in, she saw the stories.

The waiting.

The hoping.

The longing that dwelled in each passing heart.

She had been among them once.

Or maybe she still was.

The Language of the Unspoken

I see what is revealed, but beyond that, I see what is concealed.

The uncertainty in a stranger's stride, the yearning
hidden between words unspoken, the pain borne in a
stolen look.
The eyes can be fooled.
But the soul— the soul never lies.

The Moment of Acceptance

She sat on a bench, allowing the evening to settle around
her.
She had spent so much of her life questioning what was
real, doubting what she felt, looking for clarity in places
that only provided illusions.
But when she saw the world through feeling, everything
made sense.
"I see it now."
Not just what was in front of her.
But what had always been present?
Most will keep on moving, keep on looking, keep on
missing the depth hidden in plain sight. But she—she had
stopped. She had learned to see.
And now, there was no going back.
Aurelia breathed out, her heart calm.
She had always looked for answers, thinking they were
far away, distant, hidden in things she had not yet
discovered.

But perhaps the answers had been here all along.
Perhaps all she ever needed to do was look.

35

CHAPTER ELEVEN

WHY I SEE

The question nagged at Aurelia as she strolled along the empty streets.

Why do I see?

Why did her heart draw her to the unseen places of the world? Why couldn't she live like everyone else—gliding along without questioning, without sensing everything so acutely?

She had once considered it a curse, to see deeper than the surface, to catch the sorrow in forced smiles, the loneliness trapped in laughter, the truth masked beneath carefully woven words.

But now, she was starting to get it.

Perhaps seeing was not about the world.

Perhaps it was about her.

The Unraveling of Perception

Some are born to move through life untouched, never questioning, never seeking more than what is set before them.
But then there are those who are born to see—to notice, to feel, to understand what others cannot.
And for them, life is not just a series of moments—it is a tapestry of meaning, woven with unseen threads.

The Thin Veil Between Knowing and Seeking

She had grown up asking questions the world could not answer.

Why did people love only to leave?

Why did sorrow linger long after the moment had passed?

Why were some hearts broken and others never knew what it was to feel at all?

The more she observed, the more she yearned. And the more she yearned, the more she understood—she was not seeking answers in the world.

She was seeking herself.

The Burden of Awareness

I do not see it because I prefer it.

I see because I have to.

Because the world speaks its secrets and my heart

cannot help but hear.

Because to shut my eyes would be simpler, but I was never meant to dwell in darkness.

Because my heart speaks a language my mind has yet to interpret.

And so l see.

And I see more and more.

Even when it hurts.

The Weight of Knowing

She breathed out, resting against a tree, the night air chilled on her skin.

To see was to sense.

To be meant to bear.

And to bear meant to hurt.

But even with the burden of knowledge, she would not exchange it for blindness.

For in the pain of seeing, she had discovered purpose.

And in purpose, she had discovered herself.

Some live without seeing and perhaps that is their freedom.

But she—she had been given sight. And though it was heavy, though it was boundless, it was also a gift.

Because in looking at the world, she had learned to look at herself.

Aurelia smiled gently, her eyes closing.

She knew now. She didn't see because she needed to, but because she was supposed to.
Because her seeing was not only about the world.
It was about who she was becoming .
And that was enough.

CHAPTER TWELVE

WHERE I SEE

The world was a map of moments—places bound
together by time, by memory, by the gravity of every
step taken.
Aurelia had walked through cities that never slept,
through small towns where time moved at a slower pace,
through woods where the wind whispered low.
And in each location, she had seen something new.
Not because the world changed, but because she did.

The Meaning Within Every Place

*Where one is standing is less a question of geography,
more a question of point of view. The same highway that
is endless to one is a commencement to another. The
same heaven that holds promise for one holds grief for
another.*

A location does not shift. It's the eyes it is seen with that change.

The Streets That Knew Her Name

She passed by a worn cafe, its warm light spilling onto the sidewalk.
She had been here before. She had laughed here once, with someone who no longer walked with her. It was the same café. The same street. The same air that filled the space between buildings.
But she was different now.
And because she was different, the place no longer meant the same.
She breathed.
Spaces do not hold us. We hold ourselves in them.

The Truth in Every Place

Where I look is not where I am.
It is where I have been.
It is where I am headed. A street is merely a street—until it contains a memory.
Until it bears the whisper of a name that once meant everything.
But time passes.
And so do I.

The Places That Felt Like Home

There were locations she never went back to, not due to inability but because she had outgrown them.

There were destinations she ached to see, not because they were unlike the others, but because she would view them through new lenses.

And finally, some destinations always seemed like home.

Not because of their walls or the streets, but because of what they had taught her.

A peaceful park where she had first known calm.

A roof where she had once promised herself.

An ocean that had instructed her to let go.

She bore these spaces within her.

And wherever she travelled, they would always be there.

Not on a map, but in her heart.

Home is a place some think. Home is a person some think. But for those who've walked the world, home is neither.

Home is the sense of belonging. The understanding that no matter where one is, they are precisely where they are meant to be.

And she—she was beginning to learn to belong to herself.

Aurelia gazed up at the stars, the same ones twinkling above her, wherever she happened to be.

She did not have to look for somewhere to call home.

She was home.

Wherever she went, she belonged.

Because the most honest place she had ever known was inside herself.

CHAPTER THIRTEEN

WHO I SEE

Faces abounded in the world, staying still in pockets of quiet, known and forgotten alike.

Aurelia had waited years for the people, taking in their body language, their unexpressed feelings, the burdens they held in their gaze.

But she never inquired who she saw.

Did she see them for who they were?

Or how she envisioned them?

The Illusion of Identity

We don't see individuals as they are. We see them as we are.

Each individual we encounter is viewed through the prism of our experience, our hurt, our need. And in that distortion, we tend to confuse familiarity with truth, expectation with reality.

*But to see someone is to take away the veil of
assumption. To regard them not for what they are to us,
but for who they are in themselves.*

The Reflection of the Self

She used to think that people were constants, that if they
were in her life, they were destined to remain.
But now she realized—that people were not fixed stars.
They were fleeting comets, wandering in and out of her
sky, leaving behind their light.
Some had come as lessons, some as mirrors and some
had never meant to stay.
Each one had moulded her in ways she had not always
known.
But she could see it now.
All the people she had ever loved, all the strangers she
had ever met, were all hers.
And she was theirs.

The Faces That Stayed

I see them still.
Not in form, not in presence,
But in the echoes of who I've become.
The ones who loved me, the ones who hurt me, the ones
who lingered too long, the ones who departed too early.

They are gone, but not lost. They reside in my decisions,
in the classes I bear.
And in the manner in which I breathe their names when
I recall who I once was.

The Ones Who Would Come

She no longer feared loneliness.
She understood that just as some departed, there would
be others who would show up with new hearts, new
tales, new affinities to be inscribed.
She would not hold on to individuals in fear.
She would never ask them to stay.
She would love them as they arrived, let them go as they
departed.
And have faith that those who were meant to stay
always would.
We do not own the people who pass through our lives.
We only borrow moments with them.
And when we learn to let go of who we thought they
were, we finally see them for whom they truly are.
And in that view, is freedom.
Aurelia did not have to know them to comprehend them.
All she had to do was look and for the first time, she saw
herself.
Not as she used to be.
But as who she was turning into.

CHAPTER FOURTEEN

I See You

The world was full of voices, movements, people who passed by one with no regard to each other.
But Aurelia had always been different.
She did not just see people. She *saw* them.
Not their words, not their facades, not the persona that they showed the world.
She saw the things they hid.

The Weight of Being Seen

To be seen is a horror, but to be truly seen is to stand with no armour, no pretence, no illusion.
Most spend their lives fading into the edges, hoping no one takes too close a look, hoping no one sees the weight they bear in their silence.
But now and then, someone shows up who does see. And in their eyes, there is no place to hide.

The Moment of Recognition

She had known so many people in her life who had left
hardly any trace but some had inscribed their existence
onto her, like a sculptor working on stone.

But the most elusive were those who had seen her before
she had seen herself.

Those who had looked beyond the carefully constructed
sentences, the practised smiles and had sensed the depth
within.

Those individuals were not mere passersby.

They were mirrors.

They were reminders that she was not a ghost, that she
was not a lost soul adrift in a crowd.

She was important. She was real. She was.

The Gaze That Pierced Through

I see you.

Not so much the way you stand or the way you talk, but
the way your soul reacts when no eyes are looking.

I see the words you never utter, the fears you never
speak, the way you shrink into the silence hoping no one
will notice.

But I do.

I always have.

The Fear of Being Seen

She had spent years concealing pieces of herself; not because she wanted to be invisible, but because she was afraid of what others would discover if they looked too hard.

But the truth was, she had always yearned to be seen.

To be known.

To be held by knowing love.

She once thought that love was grand gestures, fiery speeches, vows inscribed into the ages.

Now, she realised love was being noticed.

Without begging.

Without pleading.

Without having to demonstrate her merit.

Most hunger for attention, but what they desire is recognition. Not to be observed, but to be understood. To hear the words that they cannot say, said out loud in another person's voice. To feel, if only for an instant, that they are not alone.

And when a person sees you as you... It is not a moment... It is a homecoming.

Aurelia took a breath, gazing up at the sky.

She had searched for so long for love, for purpose, for meaning.

But tonight, she understood she had never truly needed

to be seen.

And now that she had been, she would never let herself disappear again.

CHAPTER FIFTEEN

You

The world tended to converse in distractions—loud voices, passing moments and constant motion. It was simple to get lost in it, to be another wandering soul, invisible, unseen.

But Aurelia had learned something more profound.

All that she had sought, the questions, the yearning and the answers she had found in other people —had always led her back to a single location.

To herself.

To you.

The Return to the Self

We spend our lives facing outward—seeking validation, love, purpose.

We gauge our worth by others' eyes, by the roles we play, by the heft of the expectations placed upon us.

But what if, for once, we faced inward?

What if, rather than pursuing approval, we asked ourselves: Who am I beyond what the world tells me to be?

The answer is always waiting. And it has always been you.

The Dialogue with Herself

Aurelia stood in front of the mirror again, the same image looking back.

But something was different.

She no longer looked for flaws, for gaps, for confirmation that she wasn't enough.

Tonight, she gazed at herself not through the filter of the past, nor the demands of the future.

She just looked at herself.

As she was.

As she always had been.

And for the first time, she did not look away.

The Voice That Was Always There

You are not lost.

You are not waiting to be found.

You are not defined by who left, by who remained,

By those who haven't seen your value.

You have been here all along.
And that is enough.
You are enough.

The Release of Everything Else
She shut her eyes and took a deep breath.
She had looked for answers in love, in locations, in faces
never intended to possess them.
But she no longer needed to search.
Because the answer was hers.
And it had been hers all along.
Others look for love in other people, others in the world.
But the greatest love, the truest love, the love that will
never depart—
—is the love you give yourself.
You are not a question waiting for an answer. You are
not an echo waiting for recognition. You are not a
reflection waiting for approval.
You are already whole.
And the moment you see yourself as you are, the world
will never be the same again.
Aurelia breathed out, opening her eyes.
For the first time, she did not look at a girl who was lost.
She did not look at someone waiting.
She looked at herself.

And she smiled.

Because that was the only thing she ever needed to do.

54

CHAPTER SIXTEEN

ALIEN

The world no longer felt the same.

Aurelia had spent her entire life searching for a place to call home, hoping that somewhere, somehow, she would at last feel like she belonged. But now, as she stood in the centre of all that she once knew, she understood—

She no longer fit.

She had grown too big for the spaces she once curled up into.

She had outgrown the versions of herself that once made sense.

She had become something different.

And within that difference, she was a stranger to her world.

____

The Feeling of Otherness

To change is to leave parts of yourself behind. To

awaken is to see the world through new eyes. And when
that happens, the places that once felt familiar may no
longer recognise you.
This is the cost of growth.
You will walk streets that once were familiar and feel
like a stranger.
You will see faces that once were home and question
why the connection no longer exists.
You are not lost.
You are not broken.
You are simply no longer the same person.

A World That No Longer Recognized Her

She trod the same streets, the same locations where she used to have a purpose, yet everything seemed foreign; as if she had entered some alternate reality in which everything stood still, other than her.

People would speak and she no longer belonged to what they were discussing.

Places that were familiar no longer caused the same kind of emotions.

The things which had once thrilled her, now seemed minor.

She had become a stranger to her own universe.

But perhaps, that wasn't necessarily a bad thing.

The Space Between Who She Was and Who She Is
I am a stranger to my history, a wanderer in a world that
no longer contains me.
The laughter is the same, but it does not find me.
The voices call out my name,
but it no longer sounds like me.
I am here, but l am not the same.
And that is okay.

The Truth About Growth
She had always believed that home was something
external—a place, a person, a feeling that could be
captured.
But now, she realized
The home was not where she used to be.
Home was not something she had lost.
The home was something she was still creating.
And sometimes, before one finds where they belong,
they must first become comfortable with being lost.
*Those who grow will always be strangers to the world
they have left behind.*
But that is not loss—it is change.
*You are not destined to fit into the spaces you have
outgrown.*
You are destined to step forward into the unknown, to

discover a world that fits the person you have become.
Aurelia breathed out, standing frozen under the night sky.
She no longer belonged here.
But somewhere out there, was a place she was supposed to be.
And she would get there.
One step at a time.

CHAPTER SEVENTEEN

PSYCHE

The mind was a place of infinite hallways, changing walls and closed doors that would only present themselves to the one prepared to view.
Aurelia had walked it for years, blind to its complexity, blind to the fact that within its labyrinthine and confusing pathways lay the answers she had been trying to find all along.
She had always conceived of herself as a sum of memories, feelings and events, but now she knew...
She was not her body.
She was not her feelings.
She was her mind.
And the moment she figured out how it worked, she could never turn back.

____

____

The Power of Awareness

The brain is an efficient tool, a machine made for survival.

It practices patterns, works on conditioned response and entraps us in thought cycles—unless we discover how to gain control.

Most live in ignorance of their programming, confusing their conditioned responses with truth, their fears with reality.

But those who pause, those who question, those who are brave enough to turn inward—they are the ones who are freed.

The Cycle of Thought

She had previously thought that emotions controlled her, that fear and doubt were forces she could not overcome.

But now she saw its patterns circling round and round in her head; thoughts, old scars replaying themselves like echoes in a vacant space.

All the fears, all the uncertainties, all the doubts about herself; it was not life.

It was programming.

It was a script she had unconsciously played out her whole life.

And now, she was ready to rewrite it.

The Mind's Illusions

I am not my fears.

I am not my past.

I am not the voice that says I cannot.

I am the watcher, the thinker, the builder of my reality.

And when I see this for myself, the illusions dissipate.

Breaking Free

She sat in the quiet of her room, taking deep breaths, sensing each thought come and go like waves on the ocean.

She was no longer lost in them.

She was no longer mastered by them.

She was observing.

And in watching, she had taken herself back.

The greatest freedom is not of the world—it is of the mind.

To know oneself, to look past conditioned thought, to reclaim our story—this is the awakening.

And she—she had awakened.

Aurelia sighed, feeling light, feeling bright as ever.

She had lived years locked away in her mind.

She was free now.

CHAPTER EIGHTEEN

SEEKER - REDEMPTION

The night stretched out before Aurelia, the stars twinkling like silent observers of the burden she bore. She had gone far, looked deeply and untangled every corner of herself there was still one place she had not returned to.

Home.

Not the physical home, but the place where love had ever been.

Where understanding had once been, waiting, patient and steadfast.

She had been running from it for too long.

Tonight, she would confront it.

The Road Back

*We think redemption is something we have to deserve,
something that other people give us.*

*But real redemption —the kind that heals, the kind that
restores— can only happen when we quit running from
ourselves.*

*It is not a matter of altering the past. It is a matter of
confronting it, asking for forgiveness we have refused
ourselves for too long.*

*And occasionally, to forgive ourselves, we must first go
back to those who loved us when we were lost.*

The Door She Thought She Had Closed

Aurelia stood outside the familiar door, her fingers
quivering just above the handle.

The house she had left, remained unchanged.

Time had passed on and seasons had changed, but here,
the past remained.

She didn't know what she hoped for. A fight? An
apology long overdue?

The pain of memories against her skull?

She breathed and went in.

The Mother Who Always Waited

The air was thick with the smell of old wood and
lavender, enfolding her in a silent hug. The house was

dark, soft shadows creeping up the walls, familiar enough to make her throat constrict.

And there the same chair as always, sat her mother. Eyes closed, humming a lullaby Aurelia had not heard in years.

She almost turned around. Almost let the weight of hesitation tell her that some wounds were better left alone.

But before she could move a step, her mother's voice cut through the stillness.

"You came home."

Not a question. A knowing. A truth.

Aurelia swallowed hard, taking a step forward. Her legs were heavy, her heart unstable.

"I was lost." Her words were hardly a whisper. "I thought that if I walked away, I'd have my answers."

Her mother raised her eyes then, gentle eyes confronting hers. No anger, no resentment. But a silent knowing.

"Did you find them?"

Aurelia was unsure. She had discovered things but lost pieces of herself in the process.

She knelt next to her mother, her head on her lap, as she had when she was a child. The years dissolved in a moment.

"I'm sorry." The words flowed now, let go like something she had been holding too tightly for too long.

Her mother's fingers stroked through her hair, soft,

steady.

"You don't have to be sorry. We all lose our way."

Aurelia closed her eyes. She had dreaded this moment, so sure she had been away too long to be welcomed home. But the reality was plain.

Love had never left. It had waited.

The Redemption She Had Denied Herself

I have strayed far,

searching for something I thought I'd lost.

But love is not a destination, not something that dwindles with time.

It is the home I carry with me, the echo that never ceased calling my name.

And tonight,

I have finally answered.

The Freedom in Forgiveness

They sat together in silence, mother and daughter, crowding the space between them with unspoken words.

There was no need for explanations.

No need to re-write the past.

Only this moment, this love, this knowledge that she was still welcome here.

And perhaps, redemption was not about undoing

mistakes.

Perhaps it was just about returning to yourself.

Redemption is not a bargain. It is not bestowed, nor is it achieved.

It is a homecoming. A reckoning. A moment of confronting the past and deciding to go on despite it.

She had spent years looking. But the thing she had been looking for —the love, the belonging, the forgiveness— had been present all along.

Aurelia took a deep breath, feeling the burden that had pressed upon her chest for so long at last start to lift.

She had returned home.To this place.

To her mother.

To herself.

And that, she knew, was enough.

CHAPTER NINETEEN

GOD AND THE IDEA

The night lay out before her, the stars twinkling like lost ideas across the sky. Aurelia sat under them, quiet, reflective, her heart full but wanting.

She had searched for years for meaning in love, in loss, in the ghosts of the past.

But now, another question arose within her.

What was God?

Was God a presence that watched over her, unseen but ever—present?

Was God the voice inside her who had led her through black nights?

Was God an idea—a product of the human mind, forged by faith, longing and fear?

Or was God something less?

Something she'd always known but never quite comprehended.

The Idea of God

Others look for God in houses of worship, in the scriptures, in the words of those who say they have discovered truth.

But what if God was never intended to be discovered in words? What if God was not a thing to know, but a thing to feel?

What if God was not a faraway person, but something which had always been inside us?

The God She Had Always Known

Aurelia shut her eyes and the wind pushed softly against her face.

She remembered the times she had sensed something greater than the quiet of a sunrise, the space of the sea, the touch of a stranger's kindness.

She had sensed God in laughter, in tears, in the secret awareness that even in her most desolate moments she had never been alone.

Maybe God wasn't a name.

Maybe God wasn't a rule.

Maybe God was the love that moved through everything.

The Presence Beyond Sight

God is not a whispered secret in the heavens, not a voice that speaks in enigmas.

God is the breeze that caresses my flesh, the beat of my own heart, the quiet in which I find solace.

God is not something to which I must stretch my arms.

God is something I already possess.

The Question That No Longer Needed an Answer

She took a deep breath, gazing up at the sky that had witnessed her all along.

She did not need to describe God.

She did not need to define God.

Because she could *feel* God—within the cadence of the universe, in the breath within her, in the love without conditions.

And that was enough.

Some spend their lives seeking God. But perhaps the search itself is what blinds them.

Because God is not far away, not out of sight, not to be discovered.

God is present. Here. Now. In us. In all things.

And when we quit searching, we finally start to perceive.

Aurelia smiled the night air a chill against her skin.

She no longer had to search.

She had already discovered what she was searching for.

Because God was not an answer.

God was love.

CHAPTER TWENTY

THE TRUTH, THE PRESENT

The past had whispered its lessons.

The future had once towered like an unanswered question.

But tonight, only the present existed.

Aurelia sat in silence, the burden of her journey no longer something to bear, but something to embrace. She had sought.She had questioned. She had unwound every iteration of herself, every delusion she had ever held.

And now, in the stillness of night, she asked herself, *What is the truth?*

The Illusion of Searching

For so long, we pursue truth like a vanishing horizon,

thinking it is something that lies ahead of us at the journey's end.

But truth is not a destination. It is not something that comes after decades of searching.

Truth is here. It is always been here. It is the here and now, the space between breaths, the simplicity that occurs when we cease running.

The Present as the Only Truth

She shut her eyes, feeling the heat of her breath on her skin.

The truth was not in the past; the past was a memory, interpretation or pieces of something no longer there.

Truth was not yet to come—because the future was merely a dream, an option yet to be penned.

The truth was present.

This instant.

How her heart beat steadily within her chest.

How the wind caressed gently through the trees.

How she was not waiting or lost but merely existing.

The End of Seeking

The past is a shadow and the future is a whisper.

But here, in this breath, in this silence, is truth.

I am not sure what was.

I am not what will be.

I am now.

And that is all I have ever needed to be.

The Freedom in Presence

Aurelia smiled to herself, full of a lightness she had never felt before.

She had lived all her life thinking happiness was something to be reached.

But happiness, much like truth, was never out there.

It was here.

It had always been there.

And now, she was finally ready to accept it.

Most live their lives waiting for happiness, for meaning, for the right moment to begin.

But life is not waiting. Life is happening now.

And when we understand that, we stop seeking and start living.

She was finally living.

Aurelia breathed deeply, and each breath was like the first time.

She did not fear the past anymore.

She no longer cared about the future.

Because the only truth that ever existed was this one moment, this breath, this life.

And she was finally, truly, here.

CHAPTER TWENTY ONE

Her - A Voice Within

The night rocked Aurelia in its soft arms, the stars above twinkled. The same sky yawned on and on, the same wind rustled through the leaves, the same beat of life borne on.

But she had changed.

For the first time, she was not seeking.

For the first time, she was calm.

The Moment of Knowing

There comes a moment when the seeking stops, when the questions subside, when the restless heart finds peace at last.

Not because the world has changed, not because the answers have been given to us, but because we have learned to trust ourselves.

She had spent years searching outward, hoping something would make her whole. But now, she realised...

She was already whole.

The Gentle Release

Aurelia rested under the open sky, her form settling into the softness of the ground, her breathing even, her heart light.

She had walked in storms, in silence, in every illusion she had ever held.

And yet, here she was. Unmarked by the past, unafraid of the future, resting in the only moment that had ever really been the present.

She had once been afraid of being alone. But now, she knew she had never been alone.

She had always had herself.

And she was enough.

The Final Whisper of Her Soul

Tonight,

There is no need for words, no need for proof.

No need to be anything more than what I already am.

I am not waiting.

I am not longing. I am resting.
For I have found myself.
And that is enough.

The Peace She Had Always Sought

She rolled onto her side, her fingers curling softly against the softness of her sheets, the heat of her own body enfolding her like a soft lullaby.

The stars would continue to shine.

The world would continue to turn.

But tonight, she would sleep not weighed down by the past, not anxious about the future, but simply resting in the reality of who she was.

Aurelia closed her eyes, a gentle smile on her lips.

She knew her value now.

And with that knowledge, she slept peacefully at last.

Some spend their lives pursuing peace, thinking it is something to be discovered, something to be attained.

But peace does not emanate from the world outside—it comes from within.

She was no longer lost. She was no longer searching.

She was home. She was enough. She was free.

* 9 7 8 9 3 6 9 5 4 2 2 5 3 *